Bedesten
a domed commercial building

GÜRSOY HAFIZOĞLU

Copyright © 2018 Gürsoy Hafızoğlu

All rights reserved.

ISBN-10: 605245217X
ISBN-13: 978-605-245-217-2

CONTENTS

	Preface	I
1	The Word "Bedesten"	1
2	The History	2
3	The Structure	3
4	The Types	4
5	The Features	6
6	How It Was Operated	9
7	The Functions	10
8	The Ownership	11
9	The Decline	13
10	The Bedestens Outside Modern Turkey	14
11	The Bedestens Inside Modern Turkey	18
12	The Grand Bazaar of Istanbul and Its Bedestens	28

PREFACE

Bedesten is a domed commercial building and its structure type was first seen in Ottoman times. It was used as a bazaar in the beginning; a bazaar in which clothes were sold. In the course of time also other merchandise were sold in here. Furthermore, it had other functions such as being used as a depot for safe boxes, a place for auctions, and so on. Bedesten was the center of the trade activities in the Ottoman cities.

1 THE WORD "BEDESTEN"

The word "Bedesten" is related to a cloth woven (Turkish: Bez) in silk and cotton. Bedesten was a covered commercial building in which this type of cloth was sold in the beginning of the Bedestens' appearance. Later on, antiques and precious goods were also traded in the Bedestens.

The origin of the word "Bedesten" is "Bezistan" or "Bezzazistan" which in the long run changed into the word of "Bedesten".

The word "Bez" is used in both Arabic and Turkish languages as "woven cloth". The word "Bezzaz" is used in Arabic language as a person who sells woven clothes. The suffix "istan" is from Persian language. The word "Beziztan, or Bezzazistan" means "the bazaar of woven cloth sellers". In time, this word became "Bedesten".

Bedesten initially was built for the trade of woven clothes, but in time antiques and precious goods replaced the trade of clothes.

By the 20th century, Bedesten had lost all its functions. Later on, even some of the Bedestens were used in irrelevant ways which changed their initial purpose and finally devastated them.

2 THE HISTORY

Before the Ottoman Empire, Bedesten was used as a depot in the Turkish principalities. In Ottoman times, Bedesten was evolved into an important commercial center. In an Ottoman city, Bedesten was the core and center of its commercial activities. The main covered bazaar of an Ottoman city was always a Bedesten. The big traders of Ottoman cities at that time were located in Bedestens. Furthermore, the transit trade activities also took place in or around Bedestens. The main bazaar, the group of shops were situated around Bedesten. The structure of Bedesten was such that it was closed to the outside, and the only way out of Bedesten was through the main gate or the gates of Bedesten.

In the Ottoman cities with Bedestens, the commercial centers were inside the cities. The Ottoman cities were always constructed around the Bedestens and the Great Mosques, and further developed thereon.

The Bedestens were placed in the places close to the city walls. The shops were built next to the Bedesten's main thick walls, and starting from there in a row on both sides of the street extended to outer circles. After expansion of the shops, the tops of the extended shops were also covered and in such a way that the covered grand bazaars were formed.

Most of the Ottoman Bedestens were built in the 15th century and at the beginning of the 16th century. There are few Bedestens that were built in the 17th century.

3 THE STRUCTURE

As far as construction technique and design plan are concerned, in the Bedestens there were no small shops inside, unlike Arastas.

As the Bedestens were built as the property of foundations, in order for them to remain standing, they were built of durable stone materials and bricks. The domes of Bedestens were covered with lead.

The main structural characteristics of Bedestens were that they were built of durable material, there was one gate on each wall which served as the entrance and exit, there was an empty arcade in the middle, and the shops were placed in the beginning of the arcade.

Bedesten was a building covered by domes resting on walls and pointed arches supported by tetragonal bases. The height of the cupolas is similar to each other.

The columns were made from hewn stone, the walls were from one layer of brick and one layer of smooth rubble stone.

The Bedestens with cells which are called "Mahzen" (Cellars), were ventilated through one hole at the highest point of the four-sided inner vaults. Later on the cellars were turned into shops. The Bedestens were naturally lightened up.

4 THE TYPES

Bedesten is a Turkish covered bazaar seen in Ottoman times. Bedesten is a work of Ottoman architecture. There are three types of Turkish covered bazaars: 1. Bedesten 2. Arasta (shops of the same trade built in a row or two) 3. Han (large commercial buildings with floors).

Bedesten has also several different types. Two main types can be distinguished as 1. Bedesten with cells 2. Bedesten with shops outside.

Besides these two main types, other examples can be found as follows but in any case they fall into one of the two main types mentioned above.

Bedesten can further be classified as plain and simple one, that is built in small cities which have low commercial activities. Examples of this type may be the Bedesten in Turkish city of Amasya, the Bedesten in Turkish city of Trabzon, the Bedesten in Turkish city of Bayburt.

Also, Bedesten can further be classified as floor Bedesten which is not originally built as an independent structure, and in this kind Bedesten can be situated on the upper floor. Example of this type may be the Bedesten in Turkish city of Erzurum.

Another further classification of Bedesten can be e Arasta Bedesten which has two rows of shops facing each other on both sides of the street. Example of this type can be found in the Bedesten of the Turkish city of Kutahya

One of the main types of Bedesten is "Bedesten with cells"; in this type of Bedesten the inner space is laid out by numbers of small rooms called cells (Mahsen in Turkish). These cells have doors opening into the front ways. Examples of this type are the Bedesten in the Turkish city of Istanbul (Cevahir Bedesten or called as Old/Inner Bedesten), The Bedesten in the Turkish city of Bursa, The Bedesten in the Turkish city of Edirne.

The other main type of Bedesten is "Bedesten with shops outside"; in this type of Bedesten there are no cells inside, and there are no shops inside, there is only an empty space inside and there are shops outside. Inner spaces of these types are used as Bedesten that means there are no shopping activities happening to. The shops are placed outside, along with the outer spaces of the main walls, where shopping activities is taking place. In this type, Bedesten is surrounded by shops or shops are placed in the one or two sides of Bedesten. Examples of this type are the Bedesten in the Turkish city of Manisa, the Bedesten in the Turkish city of Tekirdag, the Bedesten in the Greek city of Serres.

You cannot see Bedesten architecture in old Anatolian or Byzantine civilizations. It is a feature that can only be seen in the Ottoman-Turkish city planning wherein new planned cities, religious and commercial buildings were built in their own unique manner. These buildings were the city centers and symbolized that the cities were belonged to the Ottomans.

5 THE FEATURES

Bedesten was made of brick and stones. And the surrounding shops were made of wood. And Bedesten height was always taller than those shops. So it could easily be distinguished. Bedesten was the essence of Turkish commercial areas in city planning.

Bedesten with high stone body and domes was like an inner city wall and can be seen from far away.

Commonly there was one gate on each wall, but the number can be changed as per structure plan. In a small Bedesten, there were two gates, and in big ones, there were four gates.

The gates were the only connection with surroundings. They were made of iron, or ebony tree and there were decorations on them.

The Iron Gate of the Sandal Bedesten in Istanbul.
Photo taken on 27 December 2017 by the author.

The domes of the Cevahir Bedesten in Istanbul.
Photo taken on 03 February 2018 by the author.

6 HOW IT WAS OPERATED

Since valuable merchandise were traded in Bedesten, at night the gates used to be kept closed. There were watchmen for daytime and nighttime separately. These watchmen were called "division head" (Turkish: Bölükbaşı). There was one "prayer head" (Turkish: Duacıbaşı) who used to open the Bedesten with praying under "praying dome" (Turkish: Dua Kubbesi) in Kayseri and Tokat Bedestens which were the only Bedestens with praying dome and other Bedestens did not have any "praying dome" and close the Bedesten in the same way. Also, there were brokers such as of today's. These brokers were doing business under state supervision. The tradesmen in Bedesten were called (Turkish: Bedesten Hacegileri) and people shopping in Bedesten were called (Turkish: Hacegan). In Bedesten apart from the tradesmen, there were people acting as safe custody agent/broker called "Bedesten Brokers/Auctioneers" (Turkish: Bedesten Dellalı). If a person was a Bedesten Broker, he could not be a Bedesten Tradesman at the same time. The Bedesten tradesmen possessed the decree of the sultan and the judge of the qadi (muslim judge) who secured the privileges. There were also the Bedesten porters that were serving for Bedesten, and they never entered into Bedesten for service. In addition there were chamberlains (Turkish: Kethüda) chosen from among the Bedesten's tradesmen, approved by qadi, responsible for Bedesten, managing Bedesten, being the head of all the workers of Bedesten, being the spokesman of Bedesten, and being the controller of Bedesten. Chamberlains were also functioning as a kind of state official that used to arrange relations between the tradesmen and the state.

Sellers of the most valuable commodities were always located inside or closest to Bedesten.

7 THE FUNCTIONS

In time, Bedestens undertaken four main functions:
(1) The Duty of Bank Service
(2) The Duty of Exchange Service
(3) The Duty of Tax Service
(4) The Duty of Auction Room Service.

As understood, Bedestens were places where there were no manufacturing activities of any kind, and only trade activities took place.

Also, caravans were organized in Bedestens on their trade journey across borders. The state records were kept here as well.

(1) The Duty of Bank Service. As being protected from thieves and fire, Bedesten was the safe box of the city. The city merchants conducted their financial transactions here too. The jewelry and the money belonging to the individuals was safely guarded here under the state protection. All the things put in Bedestens were recorded in the court registry records. The valuable imported wares, the textiles of value were safely stored and sold here.

(2) The Duty of Exchange Service. The merchandise prices used to be quoted here. The money exchange was followed in the Istanbul Cevahir Bedesten.

(3) The Duty of Tax Service. The work of taxing and tax collecting used to be performed in Bedestens.

(4) The Duty of Auction Room Service. On particular days, on Thursdays before the Noon Prayer time, with attendance of public and public figures, all the precious merchandise used to be put up for sale.

8 THE OWNERSHIP

The Bedestens were very rarely constructed to be owned as a personal real estate. Almost all the Bedestens were constructed as a real estate of a foundation (waqf). The Directorate of Waqfs in The Turkish Republic is the head of all of them. It has also regional directorates in each city of Turkey to facilitate taking care of the waqfs' estate.

The Ottoman Empire's framework was restricting private property. The foundations were institutions that allowed to retain and transfer private property to successors.

As a matter of fact, a foundation in Ottomans was established for a religious purpose of winning God's heart by performing public service and charity work. The institutions established by foundations like schools, hospitals, soup kitchens meant to develop the social life. The institutions established by foundations like bazaars, and inns meant to develop the economic life.

The role of the foundations for the protection of private property is that the goods dedicated for no purpose are now the property of God and cannot be confiscated by anyone. The founder who dedicates his/her private fortune, takes a portion of the income derived from the foundation's assets for himself and his family, and they were able to carry this right to their successors. The foundation establishment was the way of transferring the fortunes of high-ranking statesmen to their children whose fortunes had been recovered by the Ottoman Empire by the end of their term of office.

Also, broad land that was donated by an Ottoman Sultan to statesmen for a job that carries no purpose were made into foundation, and the income from these foundations was obtained by the statesmen, and this right was transferred to successors of the statesmen.

However, these foundations were also tried to be taken into state control. For example, during Mehmed II period, where the central state tendency was very strong, the foundations of Anatolia were confiscated.

Foundations functioned as legitimization and protection of the fortune of not only the statesmen but also the sultans and members of the dynasty.

9 THE DECLINE

Due to mostly opening of the Banks, and the new commercial buildings were constructed, the Bedestens had lost their functions and their tradesmen structure was damaged, as a result the collapse was inevitable.

10 THE BEDESTENS OUTSIDE MODERN TURKEY

The Bedestens were built in the Ottoman cities with a lot of commercial activities where Istanbul, Bursa, Edirne, Tokat, Ankara, Konya were coming before all else. In present time, the Bedestens remain in the cities of Bosnia and Herzegovina, Bulgaria, Greece, Hungary, Macedonia, Syria, and Turkey.

The Bedestens in Bosnia and Herzegovina: The Bedestens were built in Mostar City and Sarajevo City in Bosnia and Herzegovina.

The Sarajevo Bedesten was built in Sarajevo - Bosnia and Herzegovina in 1551 by Grand Vizier Rustem Pasha. It had 6 domes and 2 pillars. There were shops outside. It lost its originality in time.

The Sarajevo Bedesten - Oct 29, 2007 by Kathleen Franklin, Marysville CA, USA.

The Bedestens in Bulgaria: The Bedestens were built in Plovdiv City, Provadia Town, Silistra City, Sofia Capital, Yambol City in Bulgaria.

The Plovdiv Bedesten was built in Plovdiv - City in Bulgaria in 15th century. It was located near the Muradiye Mosque. It had 6 domes and 2 big pillars. It was about 18.25 x 27.06 meters size. It is destroyed completely now.

The Sofia Bedesten was built in Sofia - Capital of Bulgaria in 16th century. It had 9 domes. The ruins of the Sofia Bedesten were available until 1882. It was destroyed completely. Today there is the biggest public square of Sofia in its place.

The Yambol Bedesten was built in Yambol - City in Bulgaria in 16th century (said 1509) by Atik (Agile) Ali Pasha. Atik Ali Pasha was the Sultan Bayezid II's grand vizier. It had 4 domes, 4 gates. It was about 9 meters in width and had slim long shape. There were shops outside the Bedesten.

The Yambol Bedesten - Credit 5 July 2007 by Esm at Bulgarian Wikipedia.

The Bedestens in Greece: The Bedestens were built in Giannitsa (Turkish: Vardar Yenicesi), Larissa (Turkish: Yenişehir), Rhodes Island, Serres City, Thessaloniki City, and Veria City in Greece.

The Serres Bedesten was built in 1493 by Candarli Ibrahim Pasha (Turkish: Çandarlı İbrahim Paşa). It had 6 domes, and 2 big pillars. The domes are covered with tiles instead of lead. It had a rectangular shape. There were shops outside.

The Larissa Bedesten (Turkish: Yenişehir) was built in 16th century by Omer Bey (Turkish: Ömer). It was about 27 m x 18 meters in size. It had 6 domes, 2 pillars and 4 gates. It had a rectangular shape. It is in ruins now.

The Thessaloniki Bedesten was built between 1481-1512 by Sultan Bayezid II. It had 6 domes and 2 pillars. It had a rectangular shape. The domes are lead covered. It is in use now as bazaar.

The Serres Bedesten - Credit 31 July 2004 by Marsyas Wikipedia.

The Bedestens in Hungary: The Bedesten was built in Budapest Capital of modern Hungary. Place was called as Budin at the time.

The Bedestens in Macedonia: Bedestens were built in Štip Municipality, Skopje (Uskup) Capital of the Republic of Macedonia, and Bitola (Manastir) - City in the Republic of Macedonia

The Bedesten in Štip . The Bedesten in Štip - Municipality in the Republic of Macedonia was built in 16th century. It had 1 big dome, 2 pillars and 3 gates. It had a rectangular shape. There were shops inside the Bedesten. There were windows in the domes like the Kayseri Bedesten. It is in use now as art gallery.

The Bedesten in Skopje . The Bedesten in Skopje - Capital of the Republic of Macedonia was built in in 1445 by Gazi Ishak Bey. It had 6 domes, 2 pillars and 4 gates. It had a square shape. It was destroyed and restored in 1900 unlike its original.

The Bedestens in Syria: The Bedesten was built in Aleppo City in Syria.

The Larissa Bedesten - Credit 9 October 2011 by Ggia Wikipedia.

The Thessaloniki Bedesten - Credit 21 August 2010 by Knop92 Wikipedia.

11 THE BEDESTENS IN MODERN TURKEY

The Amasya Bedesten. The Amasya Bedesten is located in the center division of Amasya city of modern Turkey. The full name of the Amasya Bedesten is "Kapu Agasi Huseyin Aga Bedesten" in Turkish and literally "The Door Agha Huseyin Agha" in English. The Amasya Bedesten was built in 1483 by Huseyin Agha. It had 6 domes originally but it has 4 domes today. The domes were covered with lead. It had 4 gates.

The (Amasya) Merzifon Bedesten. The Merzifon Bedesten is located in Merzifon division of Amasya city of modern Turkey. The Merzifon Bedesten was built in 1667 by Kara Mustafa Pasha of Merzifon. Kara Mustafa Pasha of Merzifon was an Ottoman military commander and the Grand Vizier. The Merzifon Bedesten had 9 domes, 4 pillars, and 4 gates. It was about 30 x 28 meters in size and square shape. There were 32 shops outside all around the Bedesten, and there were no inner shops or cells. It was restored in 2006 and is in use now.

The Ankara Bedesten. It is located near the Ankara Castle in Altindag division of Ankara city of modern Turkey. The full name of the Ankara Bedesten is "The Ankara Mahmud Pasha Bedesten". The Ankara Bedesten was built between 1464-1471 by Mahmud Pasha. Mahmud Pasha was one of the prime ministers (vezirs) of Mehmed the Conqueror during 1464-1471. It had 10 domes, 4 pillars and 4 gates. It is now used as the Anatolian Civilizations Museum. The Ankara Bedesten is a sample of the Bedestens with arasta. There was a Bedesten in the middle and there were shops outside around the Bedesten. It seems like a Covered Bazaar. There were 102 shops facing each other. Angora garments were distributed in the Ankara Bedesten.

The Antalya Bedesten. It was mentioned in Evliya Celebi's writings that there was a Bedesten in Antalya city of modern Turkey. Apart from that information there are no parts that were left from the Antalya

Bedesten.

The (Antalya) Alanya Bedesten. It was mentioned in Evliya Celebi's writings that there was a Bedesten in Alanya division of Antalya city of modern Turkey. Apart from this info there are no ruins of the Alanya Bedesten that were left today.

The Aydin Bedesten. It is mentioned in Evliya Celebi's writings that there was a Bedesten in Aydin city of modern Turkey. Apart from this piece of information there are no ruins of the Aydin Bedesten remaining today.

The (Aydin) Nazilli Bedesten. It was mentioned in Evliya Celebi's writings that there was a Bedesten in Nazilli division of Aydin city of modern Turkey. Apart from that there are no parts that were left from the Nazilli Bedesten today.

The Bayburt Bedesten. The Bayburt Bedesten was built in the beginning of 17th century and its builder is not known. It had 4 domes, 1 pillar and 4 gates. It was about 17.20 x 17.20 meters in size. It had a square shape. There were shops outside all around the Bedesten. The Bayburt Bedesten was located in center division of Bayburt city of modern Turkey.

The Bitlis Bedesten. It was mentioned in Evliya Celebi's writings that there was a Bedesten in Bitlis city of modern Turkey. There are no ruins of The Bitlis Bedesten today.

The Bolu Bedesten. It was mentioned in Evliya Celebi's writings that there was a Bedesten in Bolu city of modern Turkey.

The Bursa Bedesten. It is located in the Osman Gazi division of Bursa city of modern Turkey. The full name of The Bursa Bedesten is The Yildirim Bayezid Bursa Bedesten. The Bursa Bedesten was built at the end of 1400 by Bayezid I or Yildirim Bayezid. Bayezid I or Yildirim Bayezid was the fourth Ottoman Sultan. It had 14 domes, 7 domes at each side of a row. It had 6 pillars. In present time it is used as jewelers' bazaar. It has a rectangular shape. The Bursa Bedesten is an example of the classical Ottoman Bedestens. It is a type of the Bedestens with cells inside. It had 32 inner cells and 66 outer shops. It now has 56 shops inside adjoining main inner walls. The shops are now used as jewelry shops.

The (Canakkale) Gelibolu Bedesten. The full name of the Gelibolu Bedesten is "Gelibolu Saruca Pasa Bedesten" in Turkish and literally "Saruca Pasha Bedesten" in English. It was located in the Gelibolu division of Canakkale city of modern Turkey. The Gelibolu Bedesten was built between 1436–1453 by Saruca Pasha. Full name of Saruca Pasha is Saruca b. Abdullah. He was Greek-born. Saruca Pasha was the vizier of the Ottoman Empire at the time. He also founded the Ottoman Gelibolu Shipyard and the marine base. The Gelibolu Saruca Pasa Bedesten had 6 domes and 2 pillars. It had a rectangular shape. There were shops outside. The Gelibolu Bedesten was neighboring the Great Mosque. The ruins of the Gelibolu Bedesten were available until 1952. In 1952, it was destroyed completely. So there is nothing left today. Saruca Pasha died in 1454. His tomb is in the Hamzakoy village of Gelibolu city of modern Turkey.

The Denizli Bedesten. It was mentioned in Evliya Celebi's writings that there was a Bedesten in Denizli city of modern Turkey. Apart from that there are no ruins left from the Denizli Bedesten today.

The Diyarbakir Bedesten. It was mentioned in Evliya Celebi's writings that there was a Bedesten in Diyarbakir city of modern Turkey. As per the state records, it was in use in the first half of 19th century. The Diyarbakir Bedesten was nearby and on the west side of the Great Mosque of Diyarbakir. There are no parts that were left behind from the Diyarbakir Bedesten today.

The Edirne Bedesten. The Edirne Bedesten was built in 1418 by Celebi Sultan Mehmed. Mehmed I, also known as Celebi Sultan Mehmed or Kirisci, was the Ottoman Sultan from 1413 to 1421. The fourth son of Sultan Bayezid I and Devlet Hatun, he fought with his brothers over the control of the Ottoman realm in the Ottoman Interregnum. It is located in center division of Edirne city of modern Turkey. Alaaddin was the architect. The Edirne Bedesten is example of Bedestens with inner cells. The other examples of the Bedestens with inner cells were the Bursa Bedesten, the Istanbul Cevahir Bedesten and the (Izmir) Tire Bedesten. It had inner cells on all the four inner sides. The Edirne Bedesten had 14 domes, 6 pillars and 4 gates. The domes were covered with lead. It was about 40.54–74.94 meters in size. The Edirne Bedesten was restored and today being used as a shopping center. It was mentioned in Evliya Celebi's writings that diamonds and jewelry in the Edirne Bedesten had the worth of a couple of Egyptian treasure, and that this treasure was guarded by sixty watchmen at nights.

The Erzincan Bedesten. It was mentioned in Evliya Celebi's writings that there was a Bedesten in Erzincan city of modern Turkey. It was destroyed in 1939 by an earthquake. Now there are no parts that were left from the Erzincan Bedesten today.

The Erzurum Bedesten. The full name of the Erzurum Bedesten is "The Rustem Pasa Bedesten" in Turkish and literally "The Rustem Pasha Bedesten" in English. It was located in the center division of Erzurum city of modern Turkey. The Erzurum Bedesten was built between 1554–1561 by Damat Rustem Pasa (Groom Rustem Pasha). Mimar Sinan the Architect constructed it. Rustem Pasha was Suleiman the Magnificent's Groom and the Grand Vizier. Rustem Pasha was Croatian. He was born in a village called Butmir or Sarajevsko Polje near Sarajevo. He was the third vizier when on November 26, 1539, was married to Mihrimah Sultan, the daughter of Suleyman the Magnificent. For this reason, it is known as 'groom'. The Erzurum Bedesten had 4 gates. It was an example of the Bedestens with floors. In this kind of Bedestens one floor is used as a

Bedesten. In Erzurum Bedesten upper floor was used as Bedesten. It was of the rare examples of works of the Ottoman Empire in the east.

The (Giresun) Sebinkarahisar Bedesten. It was mentioned in Evliya Celebi's writings that there was a Bedesten in Sebinkarahisar division of Giresun city of modern Turkey. Apart from that there are no parts that were left from the Sebinkarahisar Bedesten today.

The Istanbul Cevahir (Old) Bedesten in the Grand Bazaar. It was built in 1455-1457 by Mehmed the Conqueror (Fatih Sultan Mehmed). It had 15 domes and 8 pillars. It had 44 cells. It had thick gates made of wrought iron, the same as Istanbul Sandal Bedesten. There were shops outside all around the Bedesten.

The Istanbul Galata Bedesten. It was built in 15th century in Galata which was another city apart from Istanbul at the time. It had 9 domes and 4 pillars. It had a square shape. It was about 20m x 20m in size. There were shops outside all around the Bedesten. Today 2 gates are canceled and not in use. The upper sections of the facades have three windows on each facade. It was used as a depot until 1950s, now hardware shops were inside.

The Galata Bedesten - Photo taken on 31 January 2018 by the author.

The Galata Bedesten - Photo taken on 31 January 2018 by the author.

The Galata Bedesten - Photo taken on 31 January 2018 by the author.

The Istanbul Sandal (New) Bedesten in the Grand Bazaar. It was built in 1459-1461, by Mehmed the Conqueror (Fatih Sultan Mehmed). After destroyed by fires, it was rebuilt in 1550 by Suleiman the Magnificent (Kanuni Sultan Suleyman) It had 20 domes, 12 pillars and 4 gates. It had thick gates made of wrought iron, the same as Istanbul Cevahir Bedesten. There were shops outside all around the Bedesten. It was restored in 2016.

The (Izmir) Bergama Bedesten. The Bergama Bedesten was built in 16th century. It is located in the Bergama division of Izmir city of modern Turkey. It had 6 domes and 2 pillars. It was about 21,40 m x 13,90 m in size. The ruins of the Bergama Bedesten are still available today but need restoration. The Bergama Bedesten is an example of the Bedestens where there are no cells inside and no shops outside. This kind of Bedestens were built in places where there were no intense trade activities.

The (Izmir) Menemen Bedesten. It was mentioned in Evliya Celebi's writings that there was a Bedesten in the Menemen division of Izmir city of modern Turkey. Apart from that there are no parts that were left from the Menemen Bedesten today.

The (Izmir) Tire Bedesten. It is located in the Tire division of Izmir city of modern Turkey. The Tire Bedesten was built between 15th century. It had 8 domes and 3 pillars in a row. It had 4 gates. It had a rectangular shape. The Tire Bedesten was an example of the Bedestens with cells. I had cells on two side walls. There were shops inside and outside. Outside there were 32 shops all around the Bedesten. It was restored in 2017 and now being used as shopping center.

The Kahramanmaras Bedesten. The Kahramanmaras Bedesten was built in 16th century. It had 9 domes, 4 pillars and 4 gates. It had a square shape. I had a special prayer dome. It was one of the earliest examples of the Ottoman Turkish Bedestens.

The Kastamonu Bedesten. The full name of the Kastamonu Bedesten is "Kastamonu Cem Sultan Bedesten" in Turkish and literally " The Kastamonu Jem Sultan Bedesten" in English. The Kastamonu Bedesten was built in 1474 Cem Sultan. Sehzade Cem Sultan (Ottoman Prince Jem Sultan) was a pretender to the Ottoman throne in the 15th century. Cem was appointed to a provincial governorship of Kastamonu in 1469. The Kastamonu Bedesten had 9 domes, 4 pillars, and 4 gates. It was about 23.00 x 23.00 meters size. It had a square shape. It was restored in 1803 and 1951. There were shops outside. It is in use now.

The (Kastamonu) Inebolu Bedesten. It was mentioned in Evliya Celebi's writings that there was a Bedesten in the Inebolu division of Kastamonu city of modern Turkey. Apart from that there are no parts that were left from the Inebolu Bedesten today.

The (Kastamonu) Tosya Bedesten. It was mentioned in Evliya Celebi's writings that there was a Bedesten in the Tosya division of

Kastamonu city of modern Turkey. Apart from that there are no parts that were left from the Tosya Bedesten today.

The Kayseri Bedesten. The full name of the Kayseri Bedesten is "Kayseri Hancerli Sultan Vakfi Bedesten" in Turkish and literally "The Kayseri Dagger Sultan Foundation Bedesten" in English. It is located in the Melikgazi division of Kayseri city of modern Turkey. The Kayseri Bedesten was built right next to the Grand Mosque in 1497 by Kayseri Sancak Beyi Mustafa Bin Abdulhay. Kayseri Sancak Beyi Mustafa Bin Abdulhay (the Sanjak Bey of Kayseri Mustafa Bin Abdulhay) was flag officer / Sanjak Beyi in Kayseri in the time of Bayezid II. (Ottoman Sultan). It was built inside the city walls. The Kayseri Bedesten had 9 domes, 4 pillars and a square shape. There were shops outside, total 38 shops. The biggest difference of the Kayseri Bedesten from other Bedestens is that there were windows in their domes. There was also a "Prayer dome" in the Kayseri Bedesten under which in the morning the Bedesten shopkeepers used to swear that they would do honest work. It is in use now as a carpet bazaar. Evliya Celebi also mentioned in his writings that there were two Bedestens in this city but location of the second Bedesten was not determined.

The Kirsehir Bedesten. The Kirsehir Bedesten was destroyed completely in 1938; so there is nothing left today. It was also mentioned in Evliya Celebi's writings.

The Kirklareli Bedesten. The full name of the Kirklareli Bedesten is "Kirklareli Hizir Bey Bedesteni" in Turkish. Kirklareli Bedesten was built in 14th century. There are no ruins of the Kirklareli Bedesten available today. It was destroyed completely.

The Konya Bedesten. The Konya Bedesten was built in 1539 by Kanuni Sultan Suleyman (Suleyman The Magnificent). It was located in the Karatay division of Konya city of modern Turkey. It had 9 domes, 4 pillars and 4 gates. There were shops outside next to outer walls of the Bedesten. It was in ruins and abandoned in 1891. It was destroyed completely in 1901.

The (Konya) Beysehir Bedesten. The full name of the Beysehir Bedesten is "Beysehir Esrefoglu Bedesten" in Turkish. The Beysehir Bedesten was built in 1589. It had 6 domes and 2 pillars. There were shops outside next to the Bedesten walls.

The Malatya Bedesten. It was only mentioned in Evliya Celebi's writings.

The Manisa Bedesten. The Manisa Bedesten was built in 15th century by Rum Mehmed Pasha. Rum Mehmed Pasha was an Ottoman statesman being the Grand Vizier of the Ottoman Empire from 1466 to 1469. He was native Greek in Istanbul (Greek of Turkish nationality / Rum / Roman). It is located in the Sehzadeler division of Manisa city of modern Turkey. It had no pillars. It had 4 gates. It was about 42 x 10 meters in size and rectangular shape. There were 29 shops outside all around the Bedesten and there is no inner shops or cells. It was not destroyed. It is in use now. The Manisa Bedesten was also mentioned in Evliya Celebi's writings where it said that valuable merchandise were sold in here.

The (Manisa) Akhisar Bedesten. It was mentioned in Evliya Celebi's writings that there was a Bedesten in the Akhisar division of Manisa city of modern Turkey. Apart from that there are no parts that were left from the Akhisar Bedesten today.

The (Mersin) Kirkkasik Bedesten. The Kirkkasik Bedesten was built in 1579 by Ibrahim Bey. Ibrahim Bey was the son of Piri Pasha from Ramazanogullari Principality. The Kirkkasik Bedesten is located in the Tarsus division of Mersin city of modern Turkey. It had a rectangular shape, 7 domes, 2 gates and no pillars. There were 21 shops inside. It was restored in 2004 and now used as its original.

The (Mugla) Milas Bedesten. It was mentioned in Evliya Celebi's writings that there was a Bedesten in the Milas division of Mugla city of modern Turkey. Apart from that there are no parts that were left from the Milas Bedesten today.

The (Samsun) Ladik Bedesten. The Ladik Bedesten was destroyed in 1943 completely. It was located in the Ladik division of Samsun city of modern Turkey. So there is nothing left today. The Ladik Bedesten was also mentioned in Evliya Celebi's writings.

The (Samsun) Vezirkopru Bedesten. The Samsun Vezirkopru Bedesten was built in 1670 by Grand Vizier Ahmed Pasha. Grand Vizier Ahmed Pasha was Kopruluzade Fazil Ahmed Pasha who was a member of the renowned Koprulu family originating from Albania, which produced six grand viziers of the Ottoman Empire. He was born in 1635 at Vezirkopru. The Vezirkopru Bedesten had 4 domes, 1 pillar and 4 gates. It had a square shape. It was restored in 2006 and now in use.

The Sivas Bedesten. It was mentioned in Evliya Celebi's writings that there was a Bedesten in Sivas city of modern Turkey. Apart from that there are no parts that were left from the Sivas Bedesten today.

The Tekirdag Bedesten. It's full name is the Tekirdag Rustem Pasha Bedesten. The Tekirdag Bedesten was built in 16th century by Rustem Pasha. Rustem Pasha was an Ottoman grand vizier of Croatian descent. The Tekirdag Bedesten had 6 domes, 2 pillars and a rectangular shape. There were no inner shops or cells. There were shops outside all around the Bedesten.

The Tekirdag Bedesten - Credit 3 March 2013 by Ollios Wikipedia.

The Tokat Bedesten. The Tokat Bedesten is located in the center division of Tokat city of modern Turkey. It was built in 16th century. It had 9 domes, 8 pillars and 2 gates. It had a special "Prayer Dome". The Tokat Bedesten was an example of the Bedestens with arasta. It had 21 shops on both sides. It was restored in 2010 and is being used as the Tokat Museum now.

The (Tokat) Zile Bedesten. It was built in 1494 by Tacettin Pasha. The Zile Bedesten was destroyed in part and the rest is being used as a Mosque now. It had 6 domes and 2 pillars. It had a rectangular shape.

The Trabzon Bedesten. The Trabzon Bedesten was built in 16th century near the Trabzon city walls. It is located in the center division of Trabzon city of modern Turkey. It had 9 domes, 4 pillars and 4 gates. It had a square shape. It was about 19.90 x 17.48 meters size. It was restored in 2010 and now used as bazaar.

The Urfa Bedesten. It was built in 1568 by Behram Pasha. Behram Pasha was Ottoman statesman. It was destroyed completely long ago, and there is no further information about it.

The Van Bedesten. It was mentioned in Evliya Celebi's writings that there was a Bedesten in Van city of modern Turkey. Apart from that there are no parts that were left from the Van Bedesten today.

12 THE GRAND BAZAAR OF ISTANBUL AND ITS BEDESTENS

Istanbul, one of the oldest cities in the world, was the capital of the Roman Empire between 330-395, the Byzantine Empire between 395-1204 and 1261-1453, the Latin Empire between 1204-1261, the Ottoman Empire between 1453 and 1922. The areas used as bazaar during the Byzantine period, was used in the same way during the Ottoman Empire period.

During the Sultan Mehmed II the Conqueror period, the Grand Bazaar was the largest trading center with two Bedestens. The first shops in the bazaar were made of timber, and the streets were uncovered. The Bazaar was burned out many times. Only the two Bedestens survived from these fires. During the reign of Mehmed IV in 1651, the shops in the bazaar were turned into stone and bricks, and the bazaar was converted into the Grand Bazaar of today in 1701.

The Grand Bazaar (Turkish: Kapalıçarşı, meaning 'Covered Market') in Istanbul city of modern Turkey is one of the largest (40.000 m2 closed area) and oldest (1455 construction started) covered markets in the world, with 65 streets, around 4,000 shops, around 20.000 people working and around 300,000 daily visitors visiting the bazaar. The Grand Bazaar is regarded as one of the first shopping malls in the world.

The Grand Bazaar is located inside the old Istanbul within the city walls. It is located in Beyazit Neighbourhood (Turkish: Beyazıt Mahallesi), in Fatih District (Turkish: Fatih İlçesi), in Istanbul city of modern Turkey.

The Cevahir Bedesten and the Sandal Bedesten had become the hub of Istanbul's commerce, and numerous stalls and shops were built around them. The Grand Bazaar of Istanbul also included wells, fountains, mosques, cafes and restaurants.

The Grand Bazaar of Istanbul - Photo taken on 03 February 2018 by the author.

The Grand Bazaar of Istanbul - Photo taken on 03 February 2018 by the author.

The Grand Bazaar of Istanbul - Photo taken on 03 February 2018 by the author.

The Cevahir Bedesten

The Grand Bazaar's construction commenced with the Cevahir Bedesten. The Cevahir Bedesten (English: 'Jewelry Bedesten') construction commenced in 1455 and ended in 1457. The Cevahir Bedesten named alternately as 'Inner Bedesten' (Turkish: 'İç Bedesten'), 'Ancient Bedesten' (Turkish: 'Atik Bedesten'), or 'Old Bedesten' (Turkish: 'Eski Bedesten')

The Cevahir Bedesten was built by Mehmed the Conqueror (Turkish: Fatih Sultan Mehmet), with the surrounding bazaar, and was endowed to the waqf of the Hagia Sophia Mosque (Turkish: 'Aya Sofya Camii').

Since the Cevahir Bedesten was mentioned in the Fatih foundation properties taken from Byzantium, the Cevahir Bedesten is thought to had been built on some remaining walls of a Byzantine trade structure.

In Fatih's foundation registers, the first Bedesten of Istanbul, the Cevahir Bedesten is referred as New Draper's Bazaar (Turkish: Dar el-Bezzaziyet el-Cedide) or briefly Draper's Bazaar (Turkish: Bezzaziyye, Bezzazistan). Then the Old Bedesten, or the First Bedesten and now the Cevahir Bedesten name is used. The Old Bedesten was at the center of the bazaar, for this reason it is also called Inner Bedesten.

The Cevahir Bedesten, is the core and the oldest part of the Bazaar. Around it, many shops were built as well as several caravansaries or inns.

The Cevahir Bedesten is in the middle of the Grand Bazaar, has four entrances, has shops on the four sides of the outside walls, is in rectangle shape, has eight feet, eight rectangle pedestals, has fifteen domes with pointed arches in three rows, the eight small hills next to the domes are not domes, these are feeds made for lead streams. The size of Cevahir Bedesten from inside is 29,35 x 46,25 meters and from outside 50,70 x 67,30 meters. The outer walls of the Cevahir Bedesten have a thickness of 1.5 meters.

The materials used in the Cevahir Bedesten are as follows; bricks in conveyor belts, bricks in lead-coated domes, cut stones in feet, stones and a single row of bricks on the walls.

There are four gates of the Cevahir Bedesten, with modern times names 1. Used-Book Bazaar Gate (Turkish: 'Sahaflar Kapısı') (facing North) 2. Cap Makers Gate (Turkish: 'Takyeciler Kapısı') (facing south) 3. Goldsmiths Gate (Turkish: 'Kuyumcular Kapısı') (facing east) 4. Clothing Merchants Gate (Turkish: 'Zenneciler Kapısı') (facing west).

The Cevahir Bedesten is the oldest and largest building in the complex of the closed bazaar. The Cevahir Bedesten is a Bedesten with cell. The interior space is divided into numbers of similar small rooms (cells). These cells, have an opening of a door width which face to the middle section of the entire space. These cellars have no illumination, the ventilation is provided through the holes in the vaults. There are 44 cells, cell shops inside, called "Mahzen" in Turkish.

The Cevahir Bedesten worked like a bank. The people used to entrust their precious possessions, their gold, and their jewels here. The goods, the gold and the money left here were kept by the rich and reliable tradesmen. Most of the tradesmen used to operate this money, and their owners benefit from it. The owners of these shops were called merchants (Turkish: Hacegiler). When the Cevahir Bedesten was consructed, Mehmed the Conqueror conferred the privilege of the trade to the instructors so the Bedesten tradesman and merchant was called "hacegî".

Inside the Cevahir Bedesten, there were sold jewelry, gilded Indian fabrics and precious goods. The most popular craftsmen were the jewelers working on silver and jewelry. The handicrafts of the Armenian craftsmen won worldwide awards.

In the 19th century, the imports increased and the demand for the domestic fabric sold in the bazaar decreased. Later on, the functions of the Cevahir Bedesten have not changed completely and still precious goods and jewelry are sold here. Today the Grand Bazaar is still the center where gold prices are determined.

A Byzantine relief representing a Comnenian eagle is still enclosed on the top of the East Gate (Turkish: Kuyumcular Kapısı) of the Cevahir Bedesten. Some scholars used it as a proof that the edifice was a Byzantine structure, and some asserted that, this embossment belongs to another structure and have been put here later. Some historians say that by the time of Justinianus, precious things and money of the Byzantines were hidden in a place and the Cevahir Bedesten had been built on the walls of this edifice. Thus, the eagle relief legend which led to great controversy could be explained as that the Cevahir Bedesten was constructed upon a ruined building and using its existing stones.

The eagle relief on the east door of the Cevahir Bedesten - Photo taken on 03 February 2018 by the author.

According to the information received as a result of studies of Utopian Architectural Company (Turkish: Ütopya Mimarlık), it emerged that there was an older structure under the Cevahir Bedesten. The structure under the Cevahir Bedesten was discovered by Utopia Architecture using a machine called Georadar or Ground-penetrating radar (GPR) which can scan and image the subsurface by radio waves sent to twelve meters below the ground; and then by going down the rare basements and photographing they have confirmed the structure.

The Cevahir Bedesten - Photo taken on 03 February 2018 by the author.

Exit from the Cevahir Bedesten - Photo taken on 26 December 2017 by the author.

BEDESTEN

The Entrance to the Cevahir Bedesten - Photo taken on 26 December 2017 by the author.

A Cell in the Cevahir Bedesten - Photo taken on 26 December 2017 by the author.

A cell in the Cevahir Bedesten - Photo taken on 26 December 2017 by the author.

The Sandal Bedesten

The second Bedesten's construction in the Grand Bazaar started in 1459 and completed in 1461. This new Bedesten is named as the Sandal Bedesten now. In the past it was named as Small Bedesten (Turkish: Bezzaziye-i Suğra) due to its dimensions in respect to the Cevahir Bedesten; as New Bedesten (Turkish: Bezzazistan-ı Cedid), as New Inn (Turkish: Karabansaray-ı Cedid).

The Sandal Bedesten was built during Mehmet II (1451-1481) upon a place which was used as an open market area in the Byzantine period. The Sandal Bedesten and the 220 shops around it were endowed to the Mahmud Pasha II. Administration by Mehmed II.

The inner size of the Sandal Bedesten is 40x32 m. The Sandal Bedesten is smaller than the Cevahir Bedesten. It is the second core building of the Grand Bazaar. The building is covered by twenty domes supported by twelve elephantine feet of 2.25x2.63 meters and four walls of 1.30 meters thickness. The number of domes is the highest among the Ottoman Bedestens. The domes are similar to each other and have a height of 12.70 meters, the columns are of hewn stone, the walls are of rubble, the arches and cupolas are of brick.

The roof of the Sandal Bedesten was of timber and tiles, after being subject to several fires and earthquakes it was restored and masonry vaults used instead.

There are four entrances on each wall. The gates on each wall were known as (1) The Wiremen Gate (Turkish: Telciler Kapısı) in the east, (2) The Carvers Gate (Turkish: Hakkaklar Kapısı) in the west, (3) The Craftsmen Gate (Turkish: Zanaatçılar Kapısı) in the north, (4) The Tentmakers Gate (Turkish: Çadırcılar Kapısı) in the south.

The Sandal Bedesten's nomenclature is related to a kind of cloth woven in silk and cotton, which used to be sold here. In the Bazaar in any trade there was only one price which was the right price, because bargaining in the Muslim trades was a shame. In the middle of the 19th century, the Sandal Bedesten was affected by the collapse of the local textile industry. As European industry took power that time, the Ottoman Empire's customs was decreased. Even artisan's order was removed by 1912, which enforced the Sandal Bedesten's transformation by the municipality to an auction room.

The Sandal Bedesten - Photo taken on 03 February 2018 by the author.

The Sandal Bedesten - Photo taken on 27 December 2017 by the author.

The Sandal Bedesten - Photo taken on 03 February 2018 by the author.

The Sandal Bedesten - Photo taken on 03 February 2018 by the author.

The Sandal Bedesten - Photo taken on 27 December 2017 by the author.

The list of the gates in the Grand Bazaar, Istanbul

1. Osmanieh Light Gate (Turkish: 'Nur-u Osmaniye Kapısı'). It is a very crowded door. It is one of the two gates with epitaph/panel.
2. Furriers Gate (Turkish: 'Kürkçüler Kapısı'). It is in medium size, and not a very busy door.
3. Ladder Gate (Turkish: 'Merdivenli Kapı'). It is a quiet and small door. The door is connected to the bazaar with stairs.
4. Tufted Inn Gate (Turkish: 'Sorguçlu Han Kapısı'). It is a small and quiet gate.
5. Bazaar Door Gate (Turkish: 'Çarşıkapı Kapısı'). It is one of the crowded and large gates.
6. Road Passing Inn Gate (Turkish: 'Yolgeçen Han Kapısı'). It is a quiet and small gate. It is connected to the bazaar in five steps.
7. Bayezid Gate (Turkish: 'Beyazıt Kapısı'). It is a crowded and big door.
8. Hadji Husnu Gate (Turkish: 'Hacı Hüsnü Kapısı'). It is a small and quiet gate.
9. Tarboosh/Fez Sellers Gate (Turkish: 'Fesçiler Kapısı'). It is a crowded door. It is one of the two gates with epitaph/panel.
10. Basement Inn Gate (Turkish: 'Bodrum Han Kapısı'). It is a small and quiet gate.
11. Quilt Makers Gate (Turkish: 'Yorgancılar Kapısı'). It is a small and quiet gate.
12. Lutfullah Gate (Turkish: 'Lütfullah Kapısı'). It is a quiet and small gate. It is connected to the bazaar in five steps.
13. Armorer Inn Gate (Turkish: 'Cebeci Han Kapısı'). It is a quiet and small gate. It is connected to the bazaar in seven steps.
14. Knitters Gate (Turkish: 'Örücüler Kapısı'). It is a crowded and big door.
15. Traders Gate (Turkish: 'Tacirler Kapısı'). It is a quiet and big gate. It is connected to the bazaar in one step.
16. Coral Gate (Turkish: 'Mercan Kapısı'). It is a quiet and big gate. It is connected to the bazaar in one step.
17. Rooms In A Row Gate (Turkish: 'Sıraodalar Kapısı'). It is a quiet and small gate. It is connected to the bazaar in three steps.
18. Mahmud Pasha Gate (Turkish: 'Mahmutpaşa Kapısı'). It is a crowded and big gate.
19. Broadcloth Seller Inn Gate (Turkish: 'Çuhacı Han Kapısı'). It is a quiet and big gate.
20. Swordsmen Gate (Turkish: 'Kılıççılar Kapısı'). It is a quiet and big gate.
21. Silk Cotton Fabric/Sandal Bedesten Gate (Turkish: 'Sandal

Bedesteni Kapısı'). It is a quiet and big gate.

The list of the hans (Khans/Inns) in the Grand Bazaar, Istanbul

The Caravanserais called Inns, or Hans, or Khans were motels in the Seljuks time. The hans are of the two types; commercial and hospitality hans. After the Mehmed II. (1451-1481) period, around the bazaar, passenger and commercial hans were built for sheltering of animals, for people to stay and trade. The existing inns are usually of single and double floors. From these hans the two-story ones' lower floors were for sales, service and storage, and the upper floors were used as offices. There are sixteen hans in the grand bazaar today. Only the four have gates to outside, and the rest have gates opening into the grand bazaar.

1. Agha Inn (Turkish: 'Ağa Han'). Entrance is provided through the Grand Bazaar, so there is no connection to the outside. There is only one entry. There are fountains and trees in the courtyard. It has one and two storeys and has an area of 750m². Retail and wholesale clothing stores are available. Upper floors are used as warehouse and workshop.
2. Inner Liner Tailor Inn (Turkish: 'Astarcı Han'). Entrance is provided through the Grand Bazaar. Therefore, there is no connection to the outside. There is only one entry. There are trees and fountains in its yard. It has one and two floors and has an area of approximately 900m². There are various commodities being sold here.
3. Basement Inn (Turkish: 'Bodrum Han'). It has one gate opening to the outside and there is one entrance to the inn from inside the bazaar. It is one of the oldest inns of the Grand Bazaar. There are trees and fountains in his yard. This inn is of two and three storeys, and has an area of 1,542m². In general, clothes are sold here.
4. Big Saffron Inn (Turkish: 'Büyük Safran Han'). Entrance is provided through in the Grand Bazaar, so there is no connection to the outside. There is only one entry. This two floors Inn has an area of 230m². It is used as a warehouse.
5. Armorer Inn (Turkish: 'Cebeci Han'). Entrance is provided through in the Grand Bazaar. The Han is connected to the outside through the Inner Cebeci Han. There are two entries. It is two and three storeys and it is 1330m². There are restaurants and shops selling various items.
6. Broadcloth Seller Inn (Turkish: 'Çuhacı Han'). There are two entries to the han. It has two floors and 2300m² area. There are single storey shops in the middle of the courtyard. Generally jewelry is

sold here. The upper floor is used as workshop and office.
7. Pit Inn (Turkish: 'Çukur Han'). Entrance is provided through inside the Grand Bazaar. Therefore, there is no connection to the outside. There is only one entry. It has two floors and 500m² area. In general, fabrics and clothing are sold in retail and wholesale. The upper floor is used as a warehouse.
8. Parents/Mahatma Inn (Turkish: 'Evliya Han'). Entrance is provided through in the Grand Bazaar. So, there is no connection to the outside. There is only one entry. It is single and double storey han with 425m² area. It is covered, and there is a mosque and tea house.
9. Inner Armorer Inn (Turkish: 'İç Cebeci Han'). It has connection to outside. It is one of the major big inns of the Grand Bazaar and is connected to the Grand Bazaar via Cebeci Han. There are two entries. It is two storeys and has an area of 2000m². At the entrance there were various products shops which are sold in retail and wholesale. The upper floor is used as warehouse and workshop.
10. Small Saffron Inn (Turkish: 'Küçük Safran Han'). Entrance is provided through inside the Grand Bazaar. So, there is no connection to the outside. There is only one entry. It has two floors and 250m² area. Small Saffron Khan, which has a small number of shops at the entrance, upper section is used as an administrative section.
11. Fourth-Quarter Inn (Turkish: 'Rabia-Rubi Han'). Entrance is provided through inside the Grand Bazaar. Therefore, there is no connection to the outside. There is only one entry. The Rabia-Rubi Inn has one and two storeys, is about 720m². There are small shops on the ground floor. Various products are sold in wholesale and retail. Upper floors are generally used as warehouses and workshops.
12. Moneychanger Inn (Turkish: 'Sarraf Han'). Entrance is provided through inside the Grand Bazaar. Thus, there is no connection to the outside. There is only one entry. It is single and double storey and has an area of about 250m².
13. Tufted Inn (Turkish: 'Sorguçlu Han'). It has connection to the outside. The Grand Bazaar Trades Association is located in this inn. There were two entrances here. It is two-storey han which has an area of 400 m²s. There is a restaurant at the entrance of this han, and there are small number of shops. The upper floor is used as an administrative office.
14. Gold Beaters Inn (Turkish: 'Varakçı Han'). Entrance is provided through inside the Grand Bazaar. Therefore, there is no connection to the outside. There is only one entry. It is two storeys and has a 190m² area. It is used as a warehouse.

15. Half Stone Inn (Turkish: 'Yarım Taşhan'). Entrance is provided through inside the Grand Bazaar. Therefore, there is no connection to the outside. It is a single entry han. It is the smallest han of the Grand Bazaar. Unlike other Hans, there is no retail sale and is mostly used as an office. It is single and double storey han and has an area of approximately 170m². There is a turban and a tailor shop in the entrance.
16. Chained Inn (Turkish: 'Zincirli Han'). Entrance is provided through inside the Grand Bazaar. So, there is no connection to the outside. There is only one entry. There is a tree and a fountain in its yard. It is two floors and has an 860m² area. The inn where the jewelers are located is one of the busiest and known inns of the bazaar. Upper floor is used like warehouse and workshop.

The list of the streets in the Grand Bazaar, Istanbul

1. Bitter Fountain Street (Turkish: 'Acıçeşme Sokağı'). In this street, there are sops selling jewelry, leather, suede, fur, shoes, bags.
2. Agha Street (Turkish: 'Ağa Sokağı'). In this street, there are only goldsmith shops on this street.
3. Carnelian Sellers Street (Turkish: 'Akikçiler Sokağı'). In this street, there are only goldsmith shops on this street.
4. World King Street (Turkish: 'Alemşah Sokağı'). In this street, there are shops selling suede fur gifts souvenir.
5. (Turkish: 'Altıncılar Sokağı'). In this street, there are exchange bureaus.
6. Carter's Son Street (Turkish: 'Arabacıoğlu Sokağı'). In this street, there are exchange bureaus and jewelers.
7. Mirror Makers/Sellers Street (Turkish: 'Aynacılar Sokağı'). In this street, there are clothing, shoe seller, baggier, draper, haberdashery, jeweler and bank.
8. Bayezid School Street (Turkish: 'Beyazıt Mektep Sokağı').
9. Basement Inn Street (Turkish: 'Bodrum Han Sokağı'). In this street, there are leather, suede, fur, clothing, shoes, and bag sellers.
10. Jewelry Bedesten Street (Turkish: 'Cevahir Bedesteni Sokağı'). In this street, there are souvenirs, tourist goods, carpets, rug sellers, antiques and jewelers.
11. Broadcloth Weavers Inn Street (Turkish: 'Çuhacıhan Sokağı'). In this street, there are jewelers, clothes sellers and foreign exchange bureaus.
12. Climaxed Street (Turkish: 'Divrikli Sokağı'). In this street, there are sellers of souvenirs, tourist goods and clothing.
13. Lord King Street (Turkish: 'Emirşah Sokağı'). In this street, leather,

suede, fur, souvenir, tourist goods, clothes, texting, haberdashery sellers.
14. Women Suit Like Cloak/Faradje Sellers Street (Turkish: 'Feraceciler Caddesi'). In this street, there are jewelry, leather, suede, fur, souvenirs, tourist goods, clothes, shoes, bags, texting, and haberdashery sellers.
15. Tarboosh/Fez Sellers Street (Turkish: 'Fesçiler Caddesi'). In this street, there are leather, suede, fur, souvenirs, tourist goods, clothes, shoes, bags, and rugs sellers.
16. Tarboosh/Fez Sellers Dead-End Street (Turkish: 'Fesçiler Çıkmazı Sokağı').
17. Wealthy Gentleman Street (Turkish: 'Gani Çelebi Sokağı'). In this street, there are leather, suede, fur, and clothes sellers.
18. Dry Dough Sheet Dessert Street (Turkish: 'Güllaç Sokağı'). In this street, there are only jewelers.
19. Hadji Husnu Street (Turkish: 'Hacı Hüsnü Sokağı'). In this street, there are leather, suede, fur, souvenir, tourist goods, clothes, carpet and rugs sellers.
20. Hadji Memis Street (Turkish: 'Hacı Memiş Sokağı').
21. Mr. Hadji Arif Street (Turkish: 'Hacı Arif Bey Sokağı').
22. Carpet Bazaar Street (Turkish: 'Halıcılar Çarşısı Sokağı'). In this street, there are clothes, carpet, rug sellers and exchange offices.
23. Ready Made Suit Sellers Street (Turkish: 'Hazır Elbiseciler Sokağı'). In this street, there are only clothes sellers.
24. Pearl Sellers Street (Turkish: 'İnciciler Caddesi'). In this street, there are only jewelers.
25. Coffee Shop Street (Turkish: 'Kahvehane Sokağı'). In this street, there are leather, suede, fur sellers.
26. Head of Fur Cap Sellers Street (Turkish: 'Kalpakçılarbaşı Caddesi'). In this street, there are jewelers, leather, suede, fur, gift, tourist goods, shoes, bag, texting, haberdashery sellers.
27. Smelters Street (Turkish: 'Kalcılar Sokağı').
28. Son of Karamanli Street (Turkish: 'Karamanlıoğlu Sokağı'). In this street, there are jewelers, and exchange offices.
29. Shoe Sellers Street (Turkish: 'Kavaflar Sokağı'). In this street, there are leather, suede, fur, clothes, shoes, bags, carpets, rugs, textile, haberdasher sellers and exchange offices.
30. Quilted Turban Sellers Street (Turkish: 'Kavukçular Sokağı'). In this street, there are clothes sellers.
31. Silk Thread Makers/Sellers Street (Turkish: 'Kazazlar Sokağı'). In this street, there are clothes, shoes, bags, carpets, rugs, textile, haberdashery sellers.
32. Pouch Makers/Sellers Street (Turkish: 'Keseciler Caddesi'). In this

street, there are leather, suede, fur, souvenir, tourist goods, shoes, bag, carpet, rug sellers, jewelers and foreign exchange offices.
33. Belt Makers/Seller Gate Street (Turkish: 'Kolancılar Kapısı Sokağı'). In this street, there are leather, suede, fur, souvenir, tourist goods sellers.
34. Seat Silk Thread Makers/Sellers Street (Turkish: 'Koltuk Kazazlar Sokağı'). In this street, there are leather, suede, fur, souvenir, tourist goods, and clothes sellers.
35. Upholsterers Street (Turkish: 'Koltukçular Sokağı').
36. Bearing Well Street (Turkish: 'Kuyulu Sokağı'). In this street, there are leather, suede, fur, textile, haberdashery sellers, and a bank.
37. Jewelers Street (Turkish: 'Kuyumcular Caddesi'). In this street, there are jewelers only.
38. Furriers Street (Turkish: 'Kürkçüler Çarşısı Sokağı'). In this street, there are leather, suede, fur, gift, tourist goods, carpet, and rug sellers, and jewelers.
39. Lutfullah Street (Turkish: 'Lütfullah Sokağı'). In this street, there are clothes sellers only.
40. Protectors Street (Turkish: 'Muhafazacılar Sokağı'). In this street, there are gift, tourist goods sellers, and jewelers.
41. Middle Silk Thread Makers/Sellers Street (Turkish: 'Orta Kazazlar Sokağı'). In this street, there are gift tourist goods, and clothes sellers.
42. Piece Goods Sellers Street (Turkish: 'Parçacılar Sokağı'). In this street, there are textile, and haberdashery sellers.
43. Glaziers Inn Street (Turkish: 'Perdahçı Hanı Sokağı'). In this street, there are carpet, rug sellers and jewelers.
44. Glaziers Street (Turkish: 'Perdahçılar Sokağı').
45. Tuft Makers/Sellers Street (Turkish: 'Püskülcüler Sokağı'). In this street, there are clothes, textile, and haberdashery sellers.
46. Son of the Chief's Street (Turkish: 'Reisoğlu Sokağı'). In this street, there are jewelers, haberdashery, shoes, bags, and textile sellers.
47. Painters Colorists Street (Turkish: 'Ressamlar Basmacılar Sokağı'). In this street, there are souvenirs, tourist goods, shoes, and bags sellers.
48. Bibliopoles/Second-Hand Booksellers Bedesten Street (Turkish: 'Sahaflar Bedesteni Sokağı'). In this street, there are haberdashery, souvenirs, tourist goods, shoes, bags, carpets, rugs, and textile sellers.
49. Silk Cotton Fabric/Sandal Bedesten Street (Turkish: 'Sandal Bedesteni Sokağı'). In this street, there are jewelers, souvenir, tourist goods, carpet, rug sellers and a bank.
50. Yellow Hadji Hasan Street (Turkish: 'Sarı Hacı Hasan Sokağı'). In this street, there are leather, suede, fur, souvenir, tourist goods

sellers and bank.
51. Cavalry Soldier Street (Turkish: 'Sipahi Sokağı'). In this street, there are haberdashery, shoes, bags, and textile sellers.
52. Traders Street (Turkish: 'Tacirler Sokağı'). In this street, there are carpet, and rug sellers.
53. Cap/Coif Makers/Seller Street (Turkish: 'Takkeciler Sokağı'). In this street, there are souvenirs, tourist goods, clothes, shoes, bags, carpets, rugs sellers and exchange offices.
54. Slippers Makers/Sellers Street (Turkish: 'Terlikçiler Sokağı'). In this street, there are souvenirs, tourist goods, shoes, bags, carpets, and rugs sellers.
55. Hood/Headgear Sellers Street (Turkish: 'Terpuşçular (Serpuşçular) Sokağı'). In this street, there are leather, suede, fur, souvenir, tourist goods, clothes sellers.
56. Head Tailor's Range Street (Turkish: 'Terzibaşı Aralığı Sokağı'). In this street, there are jewelers only.
57. Tailors Street (Turkish: 'Terziler Sokağı'). In this street, there are jewelers, leather, suede, fur, souvenirs, tourist goods, shoes, and bags sellers.
58. Sultan's Glory Omen Carriers Street (Turkish: 'Tuğcular Sokağı'). In this street, there are leather, suede, fur clothes sellers.
59. Flour Seller's Son Street (Turkish: 'Uncuoğlu Sokağı'). In this street, there are jewelers, haberdashery and textile sellers.
60. Large Handkerchief Sellers Street (Turkish: 'Yağlıkçılar Caddesi'). In this street, there are haberdashery, leather, suede, fur, gift, tourist goods, clothes, shoes, bags, textile sellers.
61. Gold Beaters Street (Turkish: 'Varakçı Sokağı'). In this street, there are jewelers and exchange offices.
62. Half Stone Inn Street (Turkish: 'Yarım Taşhan Sokağı'). In this street, there are haberdashery, leather, suede, fur, clothes, shoes, bags, textile sellers, and exchange offices.
63. Green Pillar Street (Turkish: 'Yeşildirekli Sokağı'). In this street, there are only clothes sellers here.
64. Quilt Makers Street (Turkish: 'Yorgancılar Sokağı'). In this street, there are haberdashery, leather, suede, fur, clothes, and textile sellers.
65. Women Clothing Sellers Street (Turkish: 'Zenneciler Sokağı'). In this street, there are carpet, and rug sellers.

The artisans in the Grand Bazaar, Istanbul from the beginning.

1. Goldbeaters (Turkish: 'Altıncılar').
2. Antique Dealers (Turkish: 'Antikacılar').

3. Lining Tailors (Turkish: 'Astarcılar').
4. Mirror Makers/Sellers (Turkish: 'Aynacılar').
5. Ornament Breakers (Turkish: ' Bozmacılar').
6. Flint Repairers (Turkish: ' Çakmakçılar').
7. Broadcloth Weavers/Sellers (Turkish: ' Çuhacılar').
8. Leather Dealers (Turkish: ' Deri Süet Kürkçüler').
9. Ragmen (Turkish: ' Eskiciler').
10. Silversmiths (Turkish: 'Gümüşçüler').
11. Shoe Sellers (Turkish: 'Haffaflar').
12. Engravers (Turkish: 'Hakkaklar').
13. Carpet Sellers (Turkish: 'Halıcılar').
14. Calligraphers Turkish: Hattatlar').
15. Embroiderers (Turkish: 'İşlemeciler').
16. Melters (Turkish: 'İzabeciler').
17. Embossers (Turkish: 'Kabartmacılar').
18. Inlay workers (Turkish: 'Kakmacılar').
19. Pencil-Opening Knife Makers (Turkish: 'Kalemtraşçı ve Maktacılar').
20. Headwear Makers (Turkish: 'Kalpakçılar').
21. Spoon Makers (Turkish: 'Kaşıkçılar').
22. Swordsmen (Turkish: 'Kılıççılar').
23. Stout Leather Makers/Sellers (Turkish: 'Köseleciler').
24. Lapidary/Jewelers (Turkish: 'Kuyumcular, Cevahirler').
25. Scissors Makers/Sellers (Turkish: 'Makasçılar').
26. Hookah Tube Sellers/Makers (Turkish: 'Marpuççular').
27. Helmet Sellers/Makers (Turkish: 'Miğferciler').
28. Miniaturists (Turkish: 'Minyatürcüler').
29. Head Claw Support Sellers/Makers (Turkish: 'Müttekacılar').
30. Book Illuminators (Turkish: 'Müzehhipler').
31. Engravers (Turkish: 'Oymacılar').
32. Shoe Sellers/Makers(Turkish: 'Pabuççular').
33. Gold Coin Dealers (Turkish: 'Rubiyeciler').
34. Bibliopoles (Turkish: 'Sahaflar').
35. Mother of Pearl Artisans (Turkish: 'Sedefkarlar').
36. Silver-Gilt Thread Artisans (Turkish: 'Sırmacılar').
37. Shawl Sellers (Turkish: 'Şalcılar').
38. Hangers (Turkish: 'Taklitçiler').
39. (Prayer) Beads Makers/Sellers (Turkish: 'Tesbihçiler').
40. Rifle Repairers/Sellers(Turkish: 'Tüfekçiler').
41. Large Handkerchief Sellers (Turkish: 'Yağlıkçılar').
42. Gilders (Turkish: 'Yaldızcılar').
43. Coffee Cup's Metal Holder Makers/Sellers (Turkish: 'Zarfçılar').

ABOUT THE AUTHOR

Gursoy Hafizoglu was born in Xanthi, Greece and raised in Istanbul, Turkey. He has a Bachelor's Degree from the University of Dokuz Eylul (Izmir/Turkey), Maritime Faculty, Department of Maritime Business Administration. He has founded the company, Bedesten Limited, a shipping firm, after graduated from the university. He works as a ship broker. He has a bicycle and once made 250 km per day with his bike. He also takes care of the cats around his office.

Get in touch with him at the web address: www.bedesten.com.tr or the business address: Atikali Mah Kimyager Sk No 11/2 34087 Fatih Istanbul Turkey.

www.ingramcontent.com/pod-product-compliance
Lightning Source LLC
Chambersburg PA
CBHW042333150426
43194CB00001B/45